Color Your Cares
Away

More Than Just a Coloring Book

Vern Mauk

BInk *Bink Books*
Bedazzled Ink Publishing Company • Fairfield, California

978-1-943837-69-4 paperback

Cover Painting
by
Vern Mauk

Cover Design
by

Bink Books
a division of
Bedazzled Ink Publishing, LLC
Fairfield, California
http://www.bedazzledink.com

Ready for something beyond just coloring between the lines?

The drawings in this book are designed to encourage the budding artist to add additional blending of colors so that the image has more dimension by adding depth and form.

All objects have a lighted side and a shadowed side. Tree trunks, for example, take on more form by adding shadow on the side of the tree or the underside of branches. Reducing the intensity of the color on the side that is in shadow gives the object a dimensional look. Gray can reduce the intensity of color, but the opposite color on a color wheel tones down the intensity in a more interesting way. Just lightly blend the opposite color with the original color. Experiment with mixing the colors to learn how much is needed of each color. Most important, be creative and have fun. The result is more than just filling in areas with color. It's a personal work of art.

A color wheel and and a color example of one of the drawings in this book are on the back cover.

VERN
MAUK

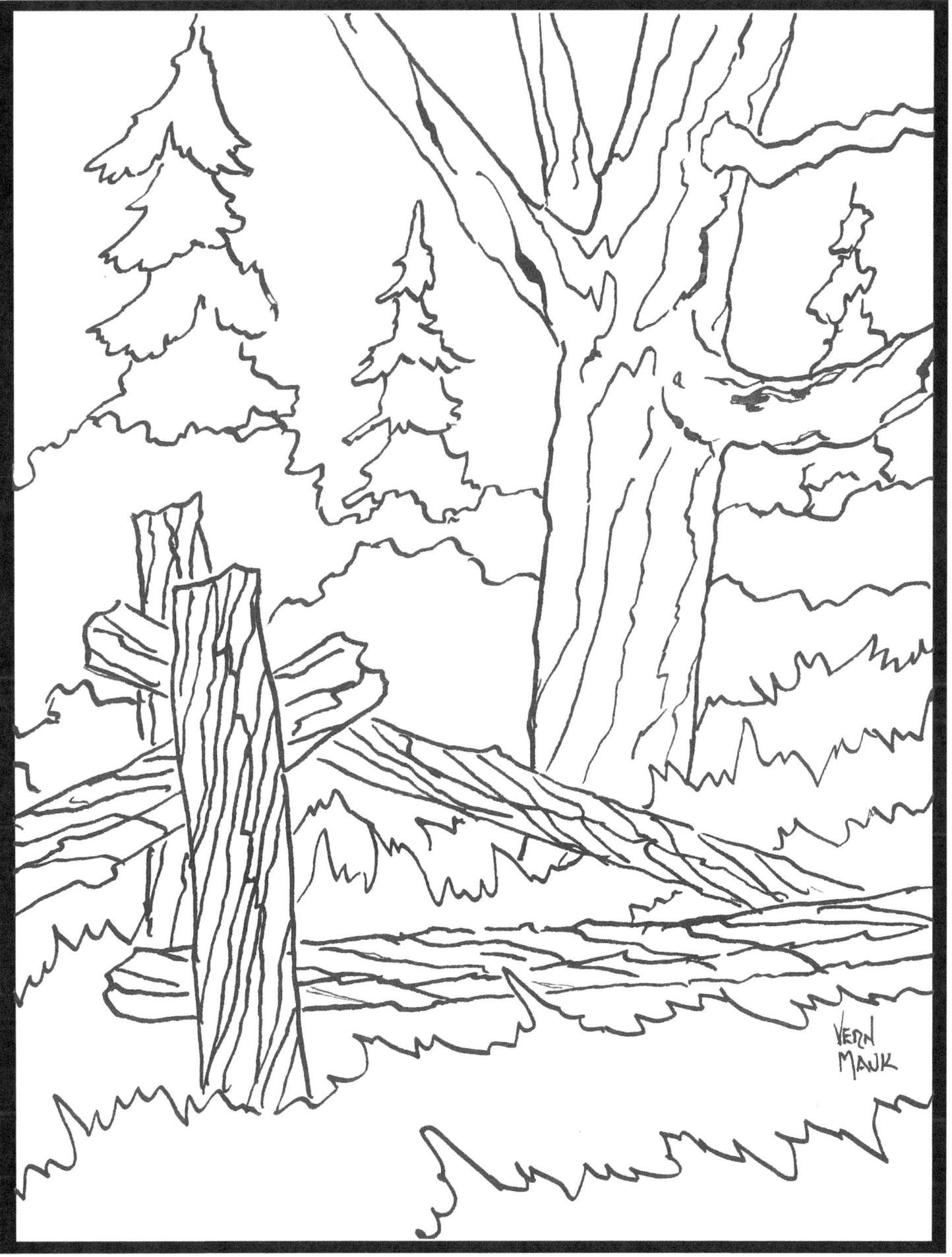

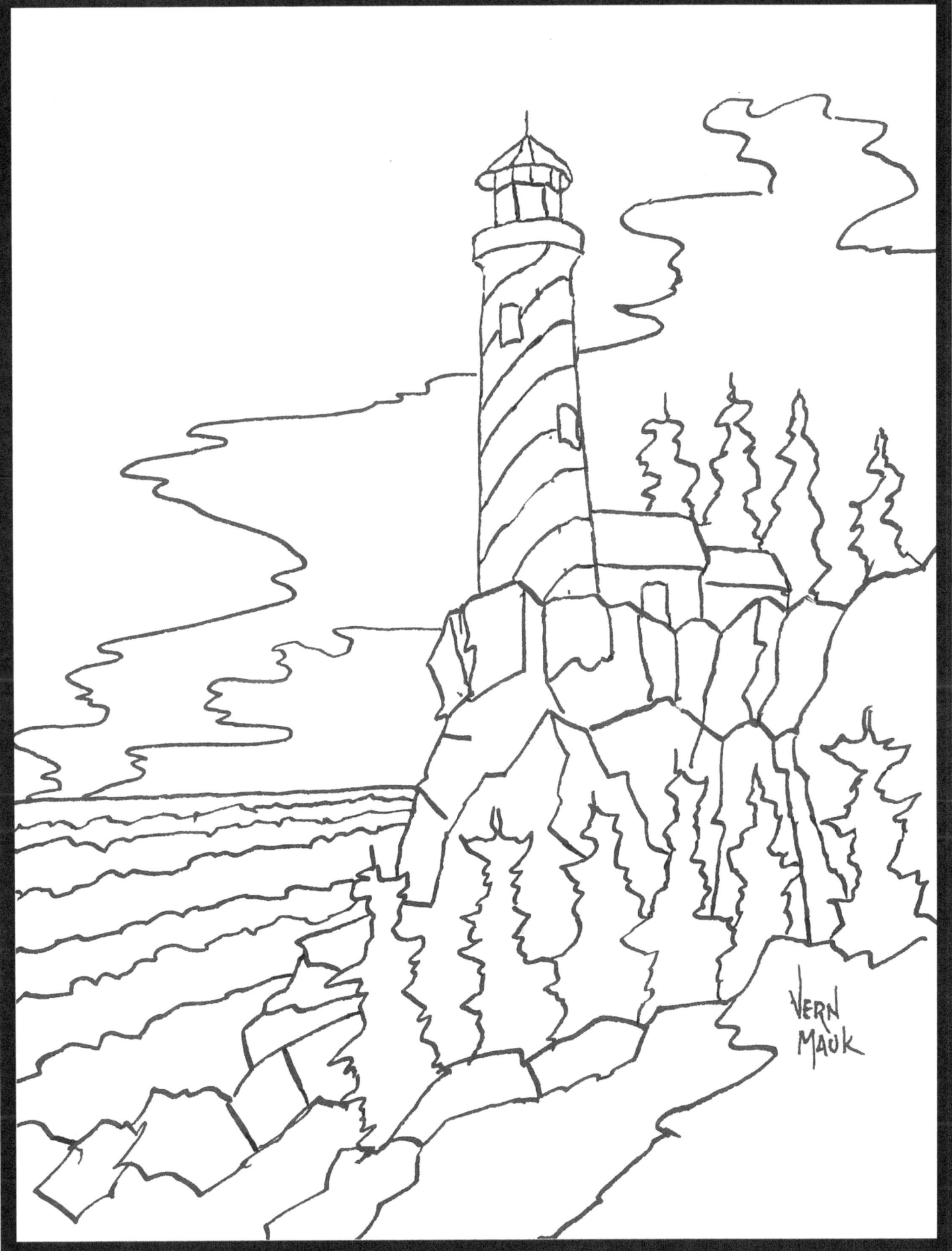

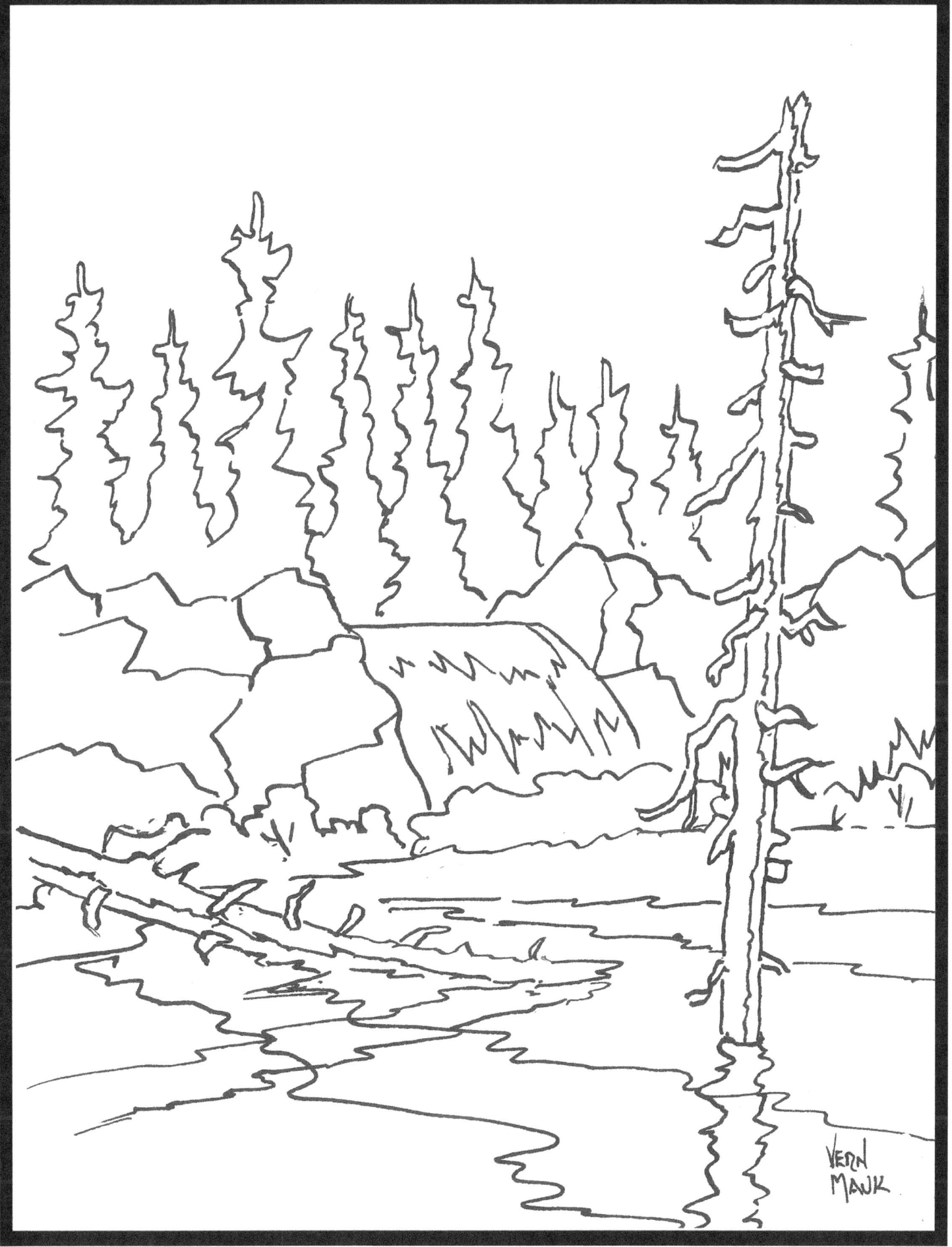

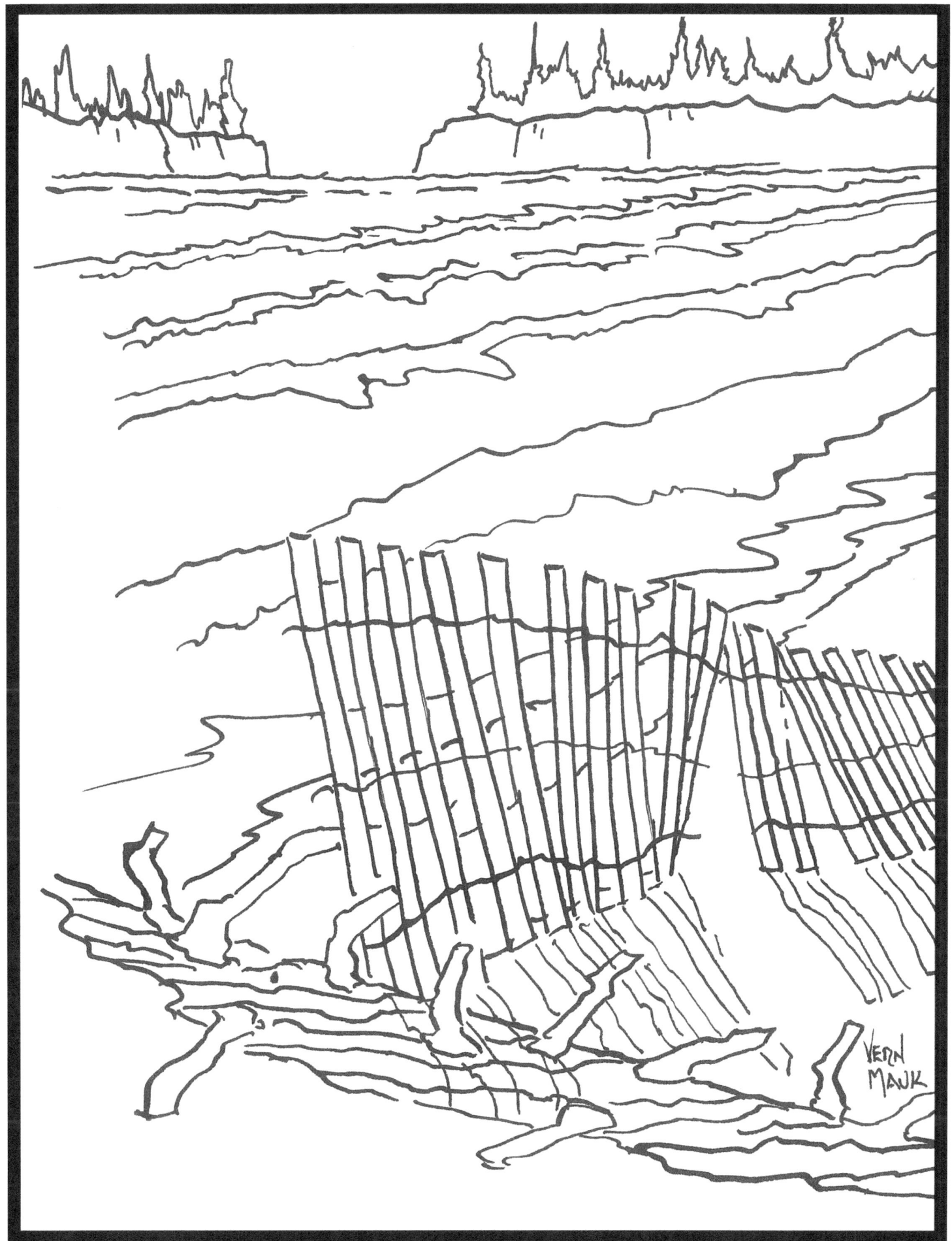

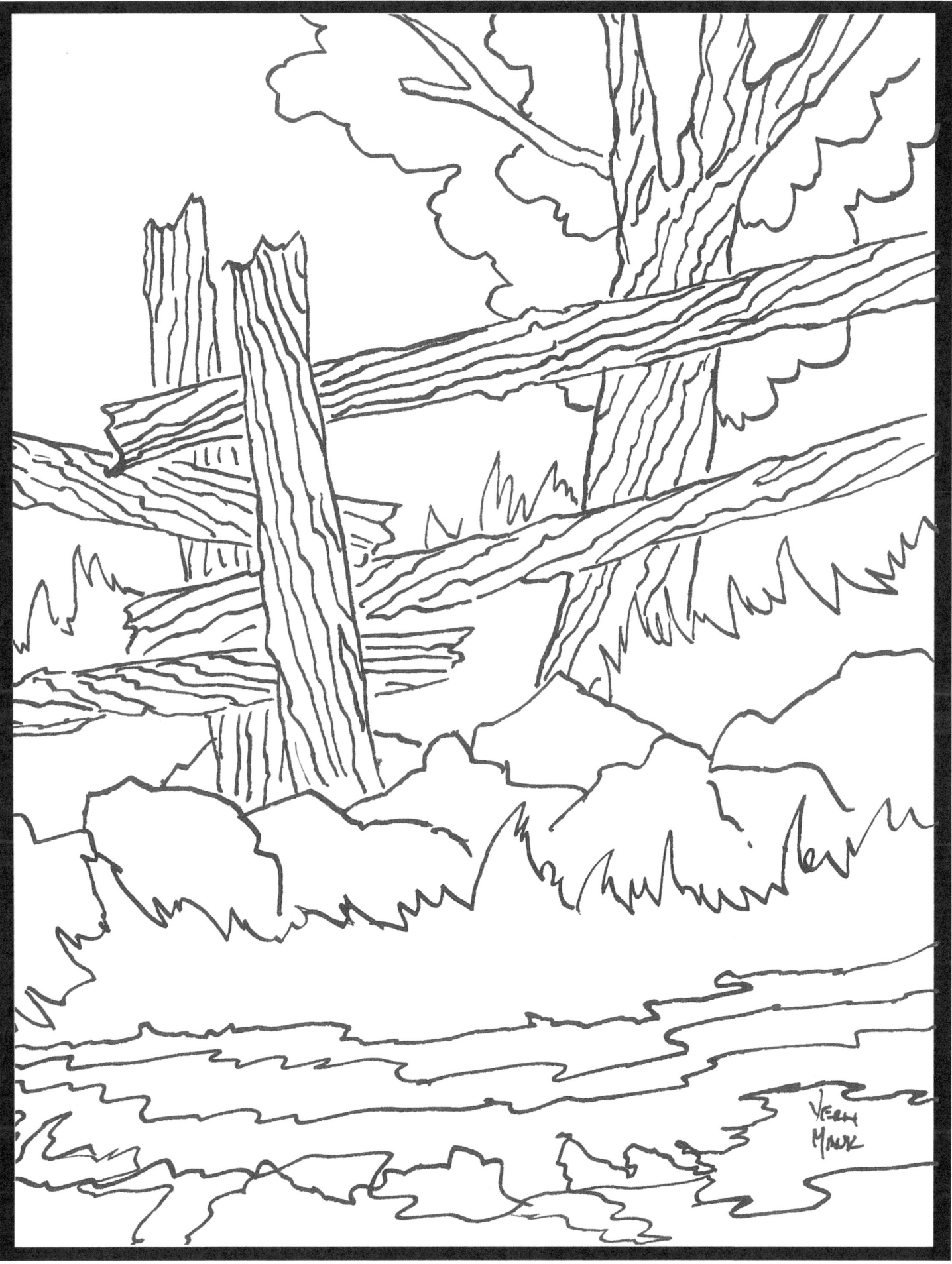

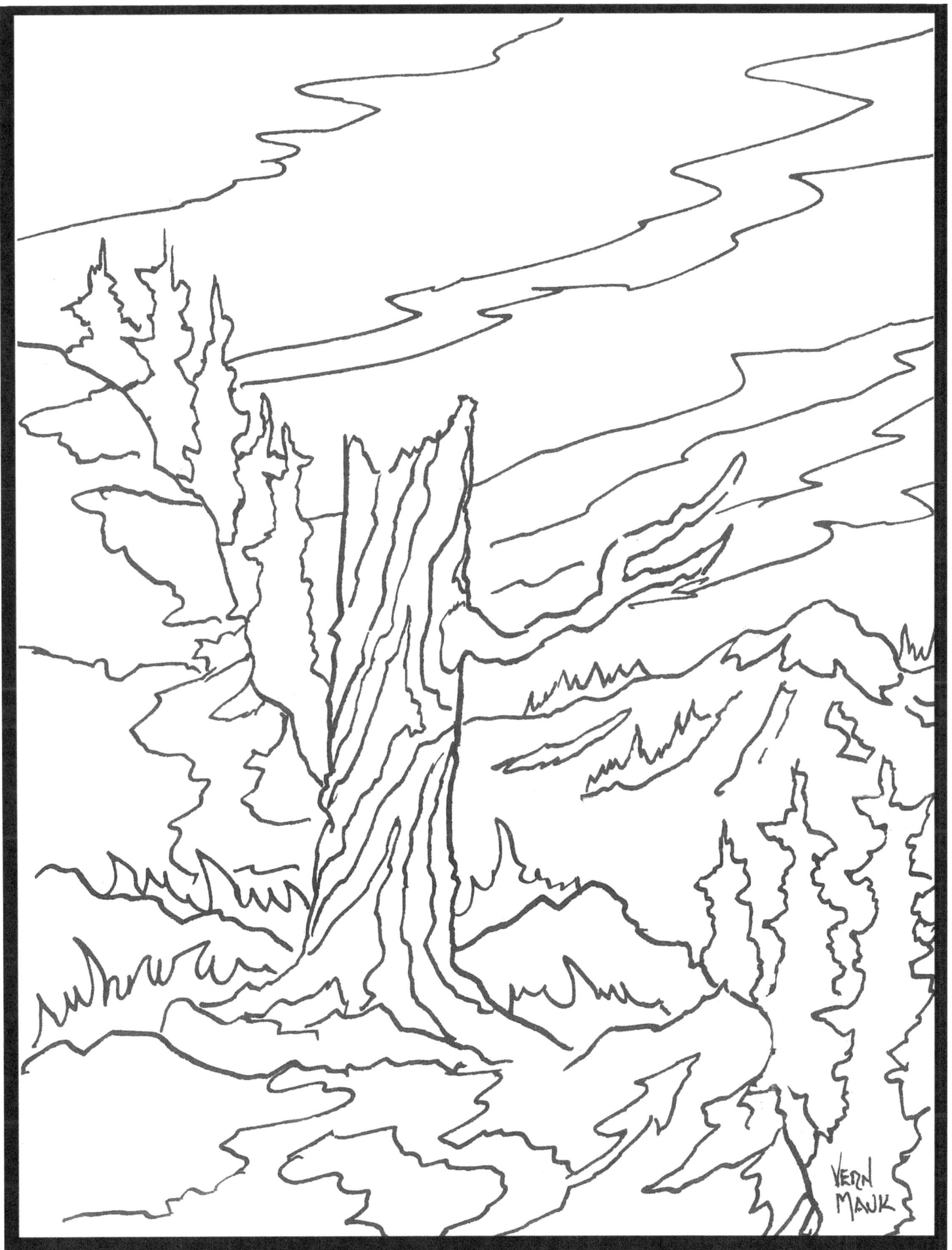

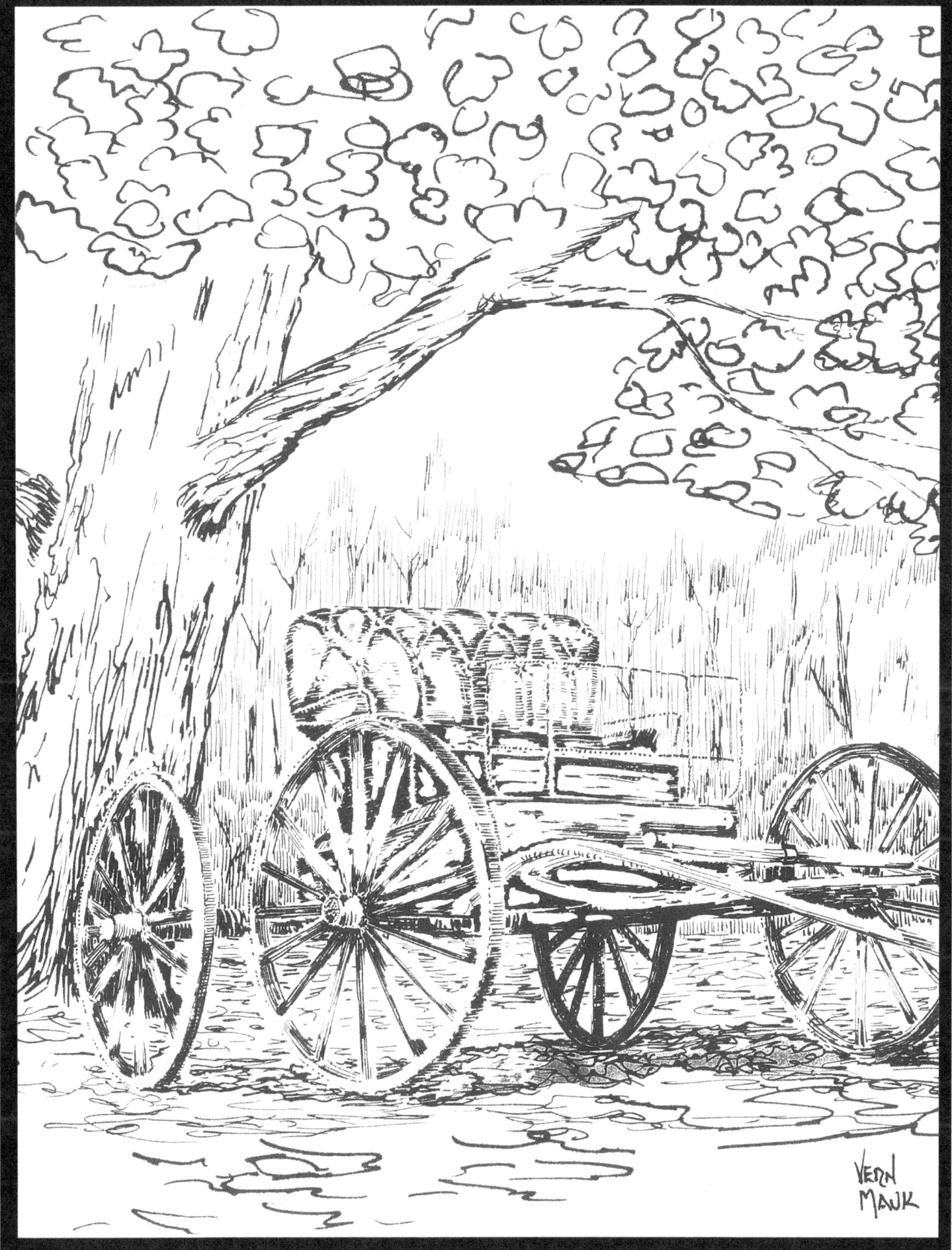

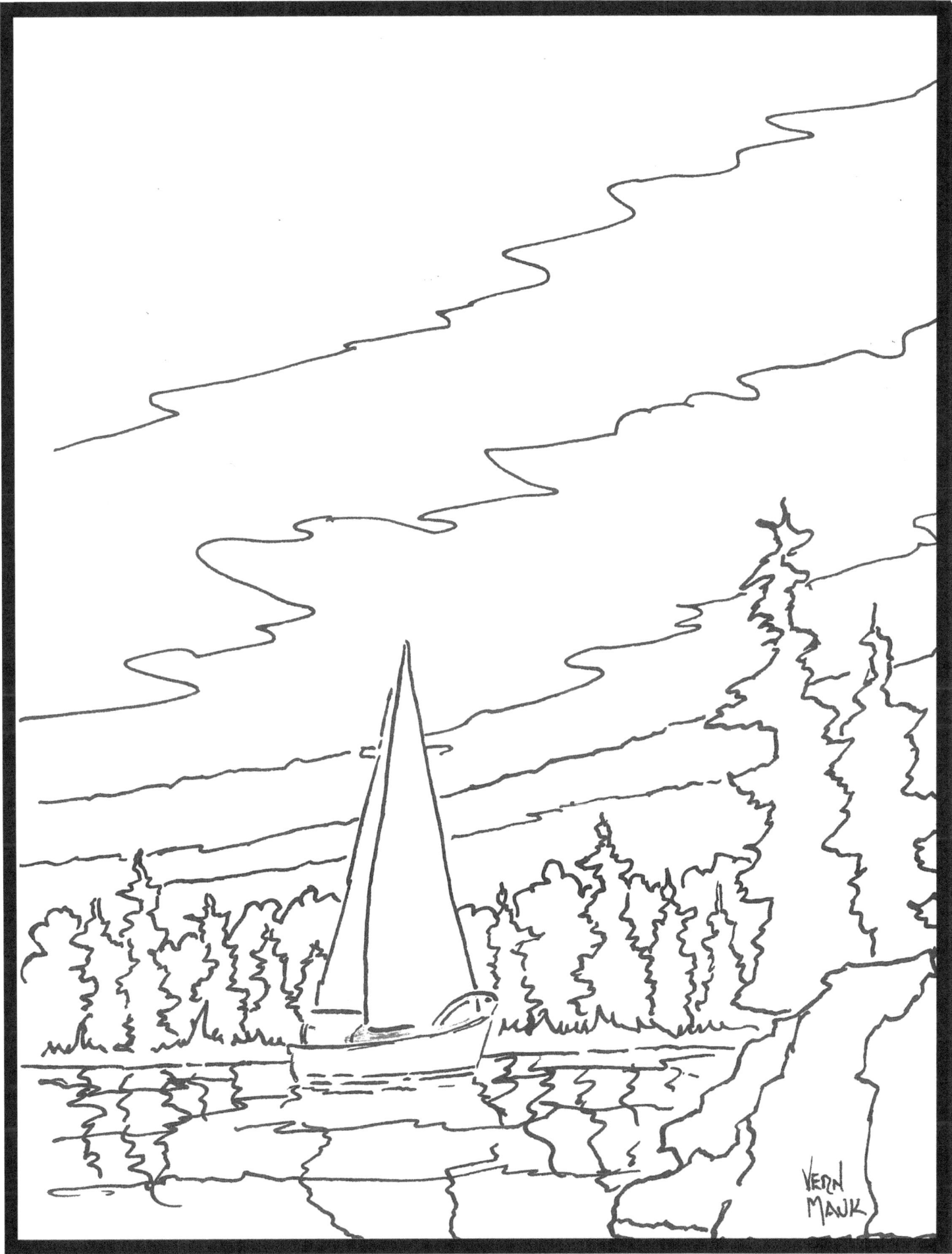

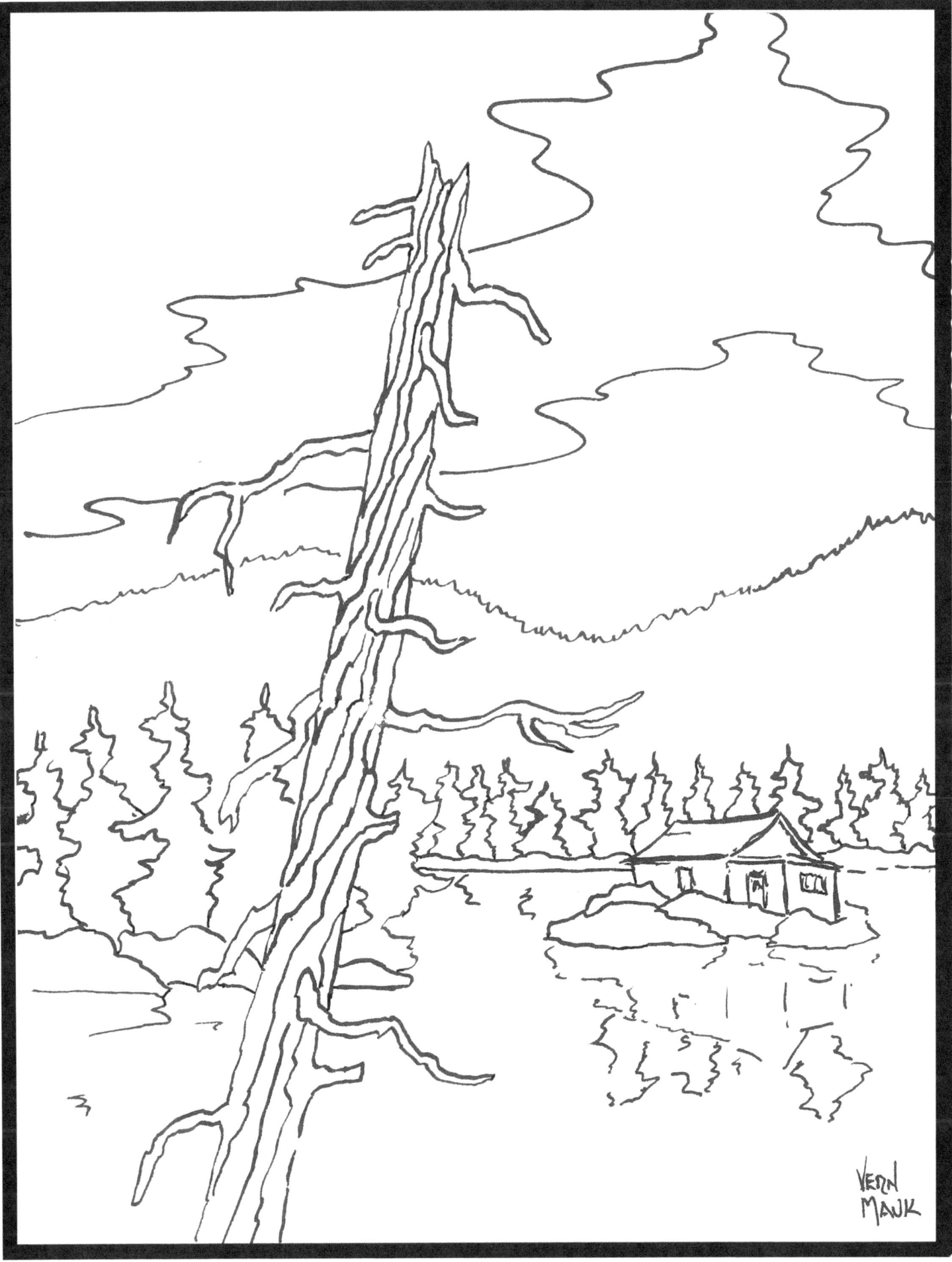

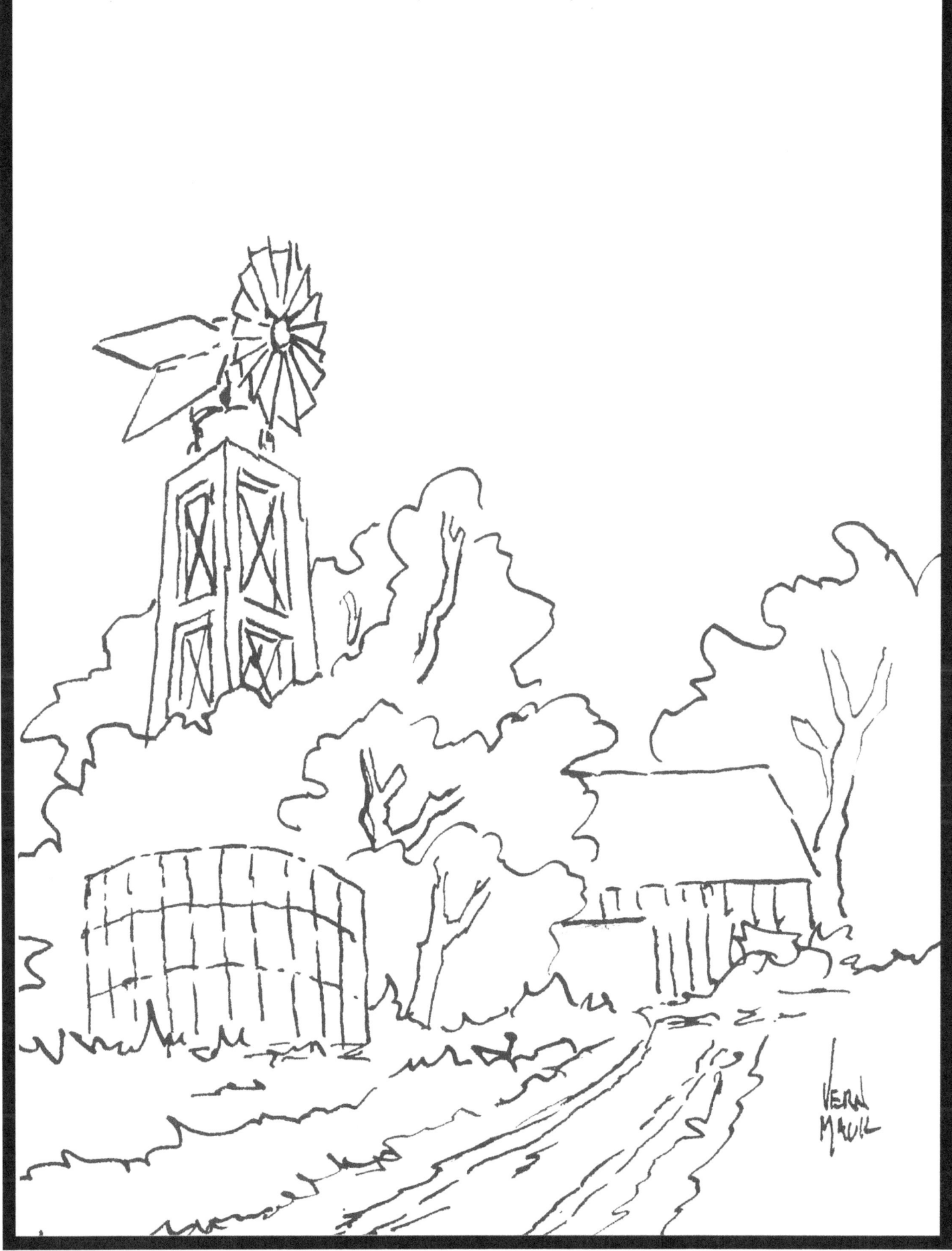

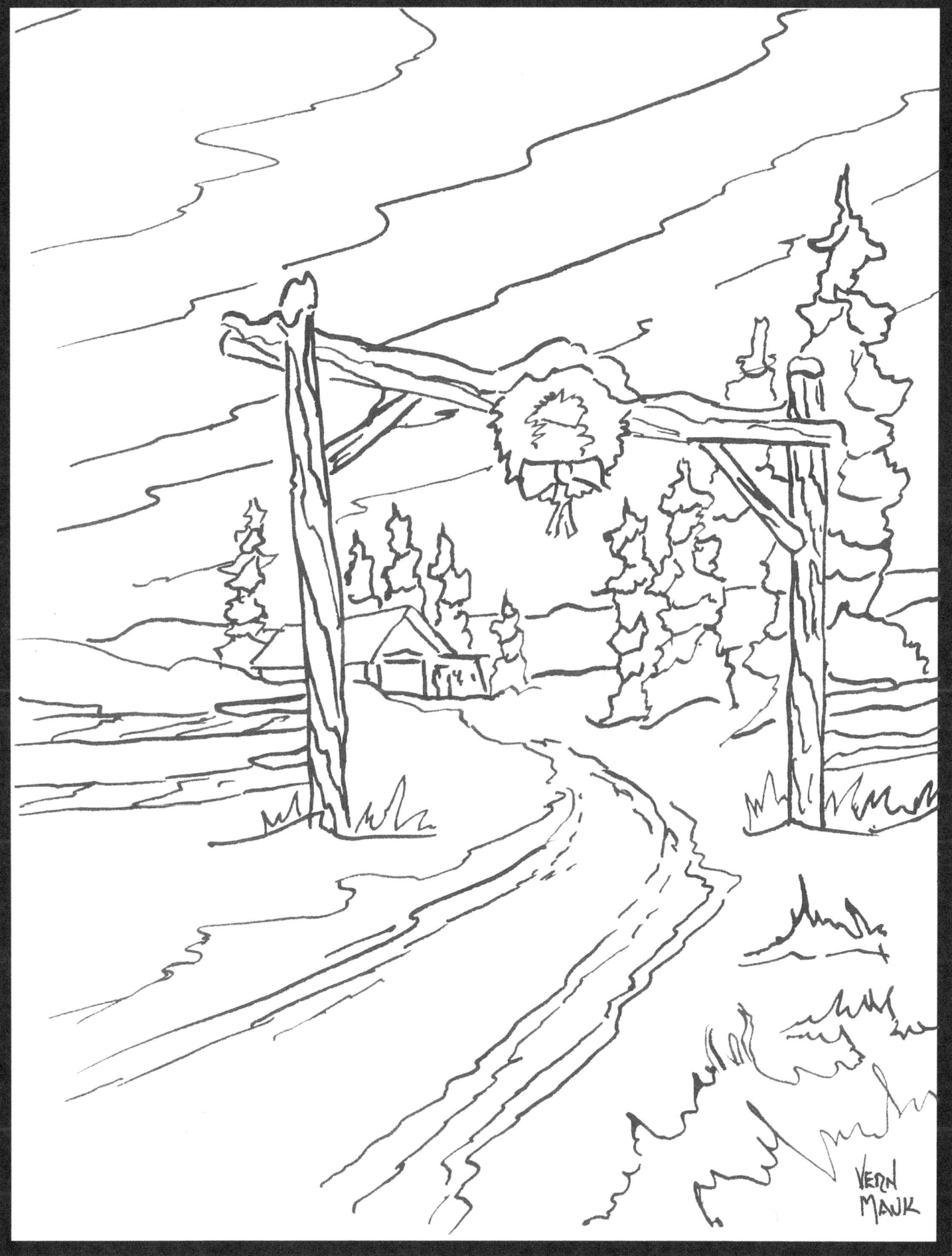

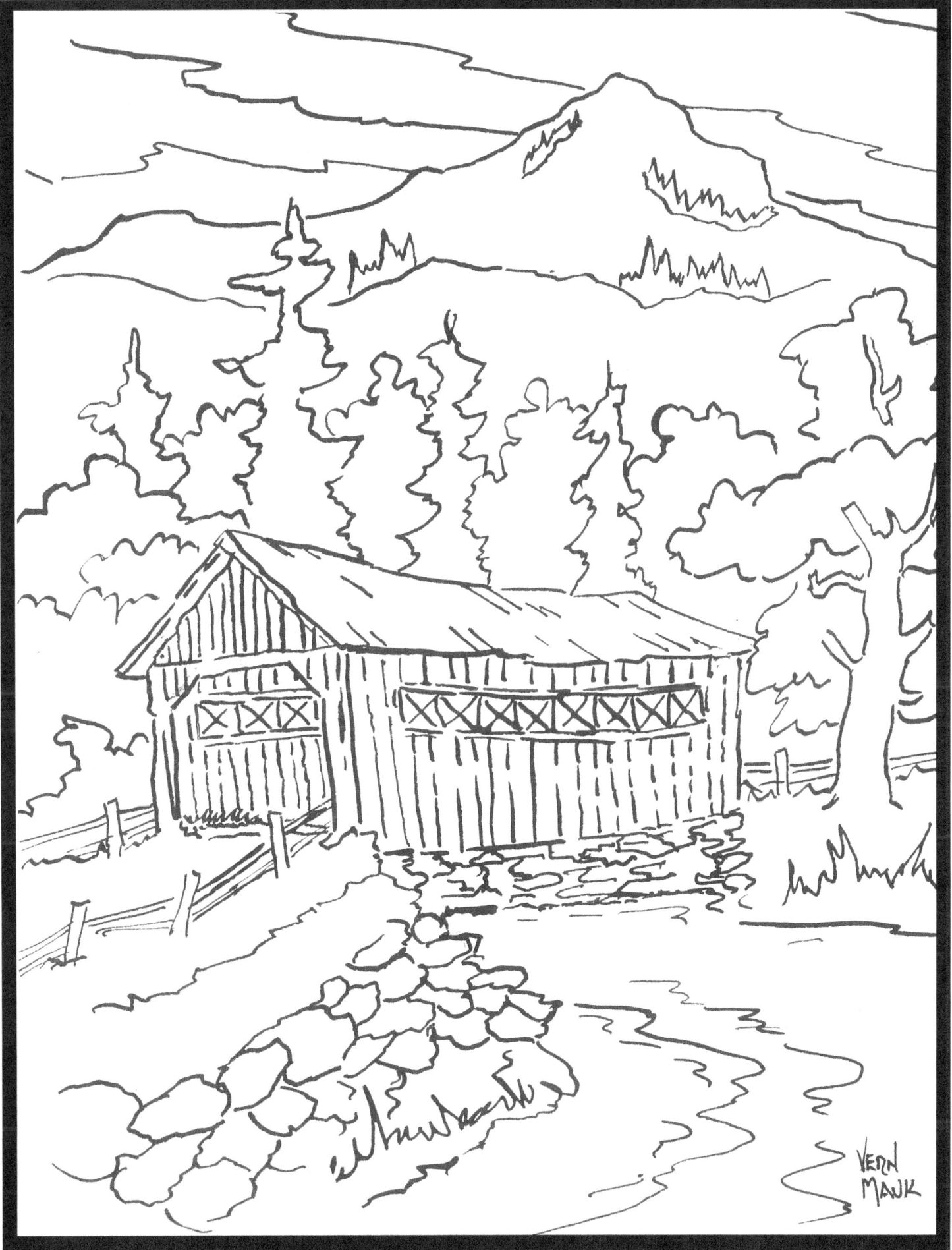

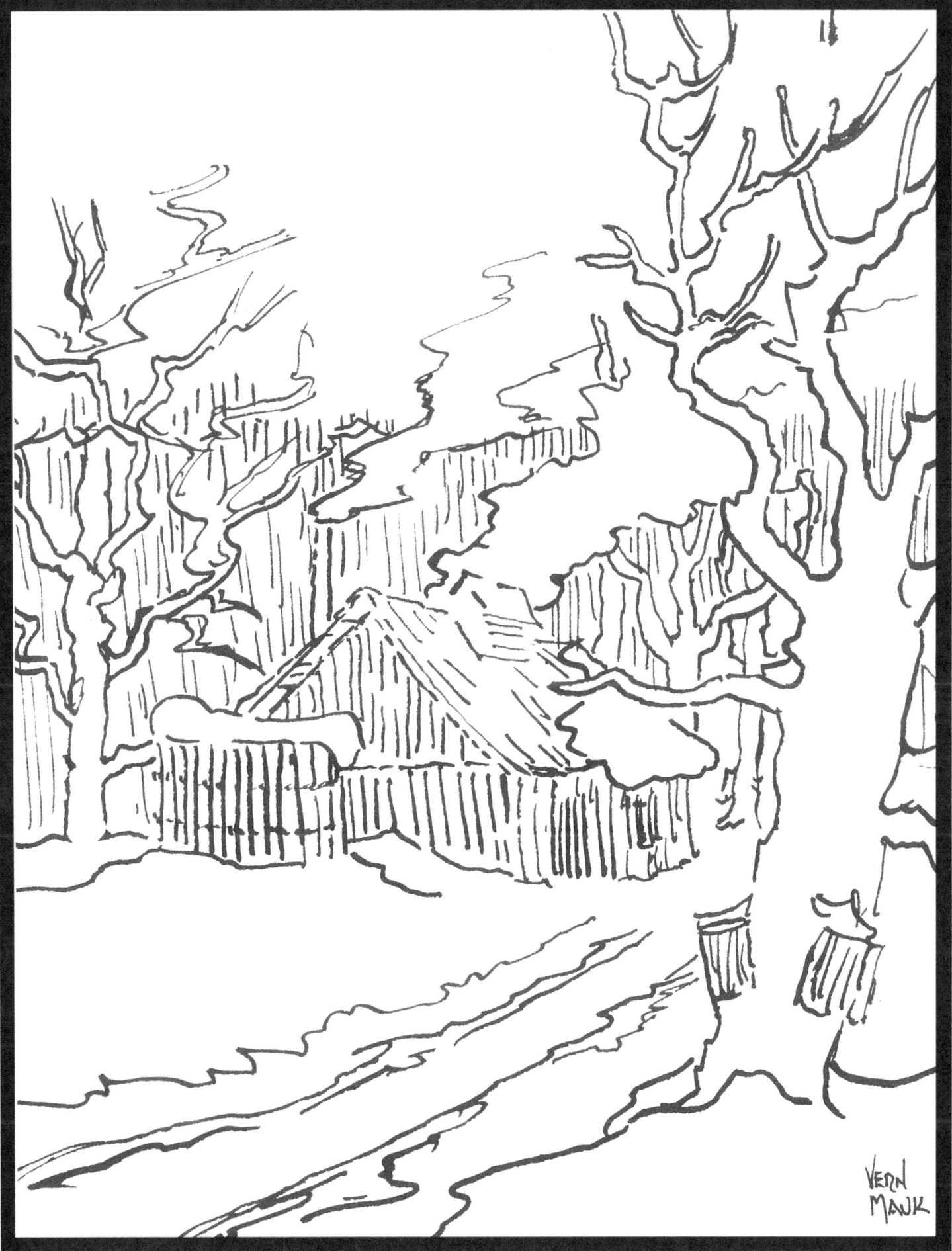

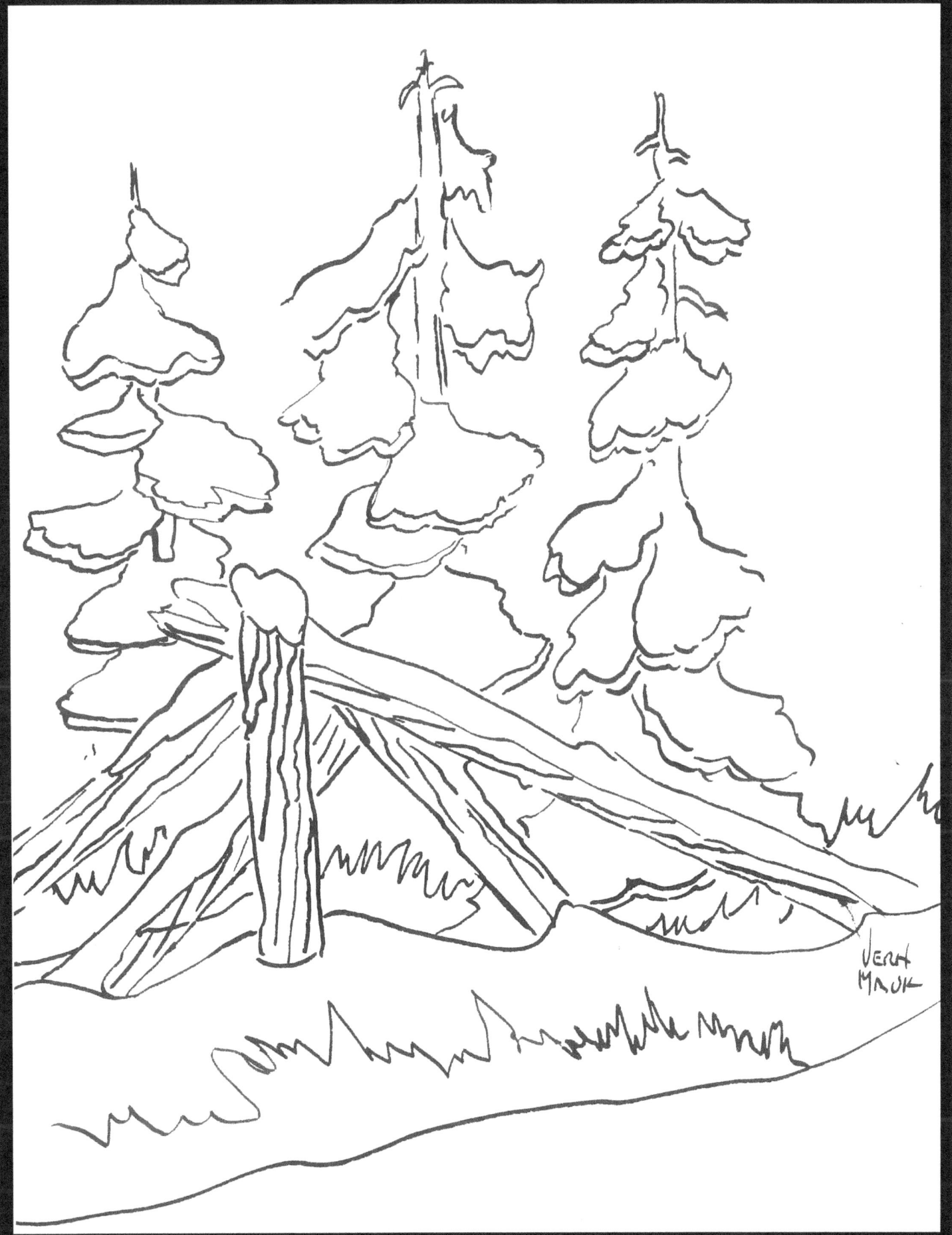

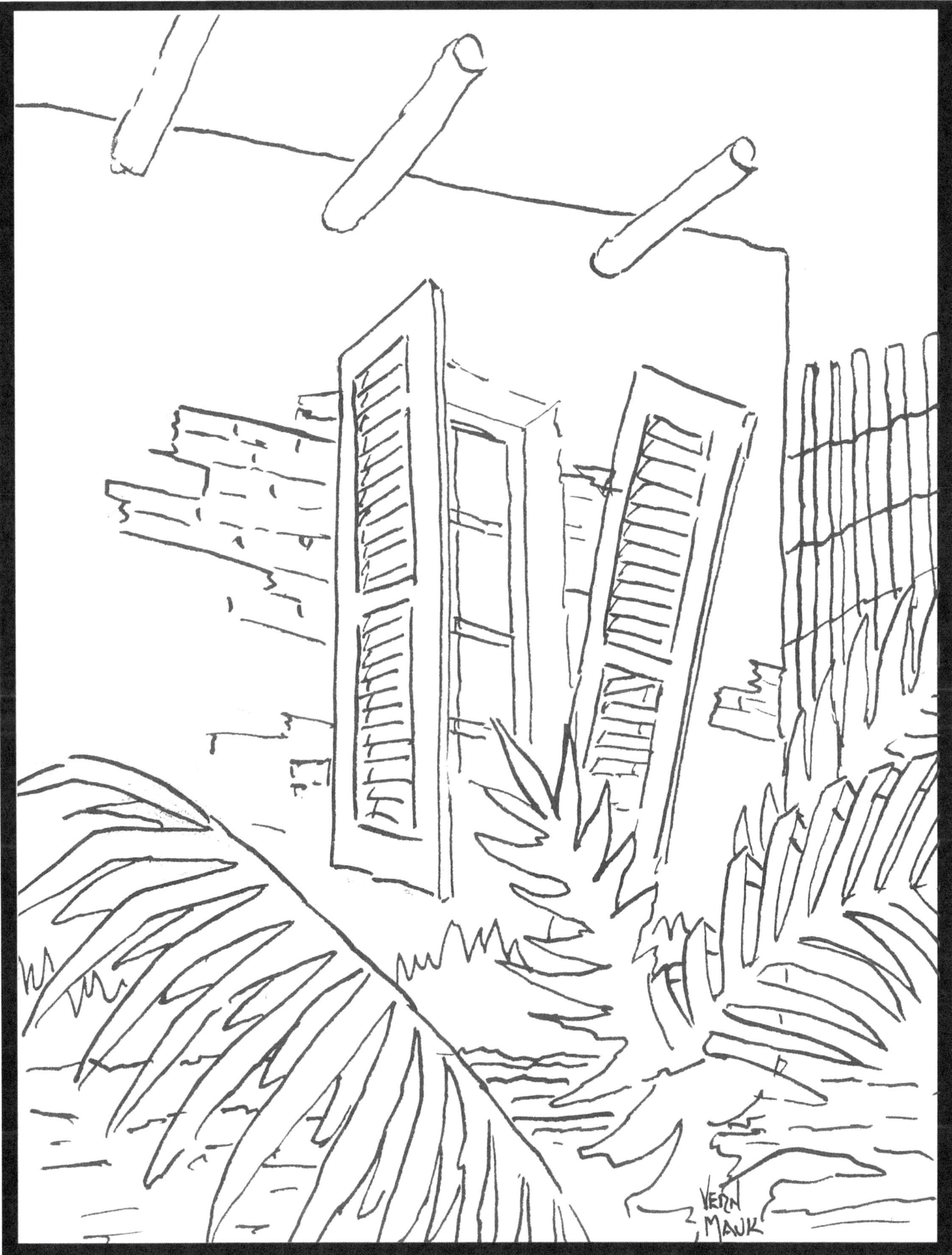

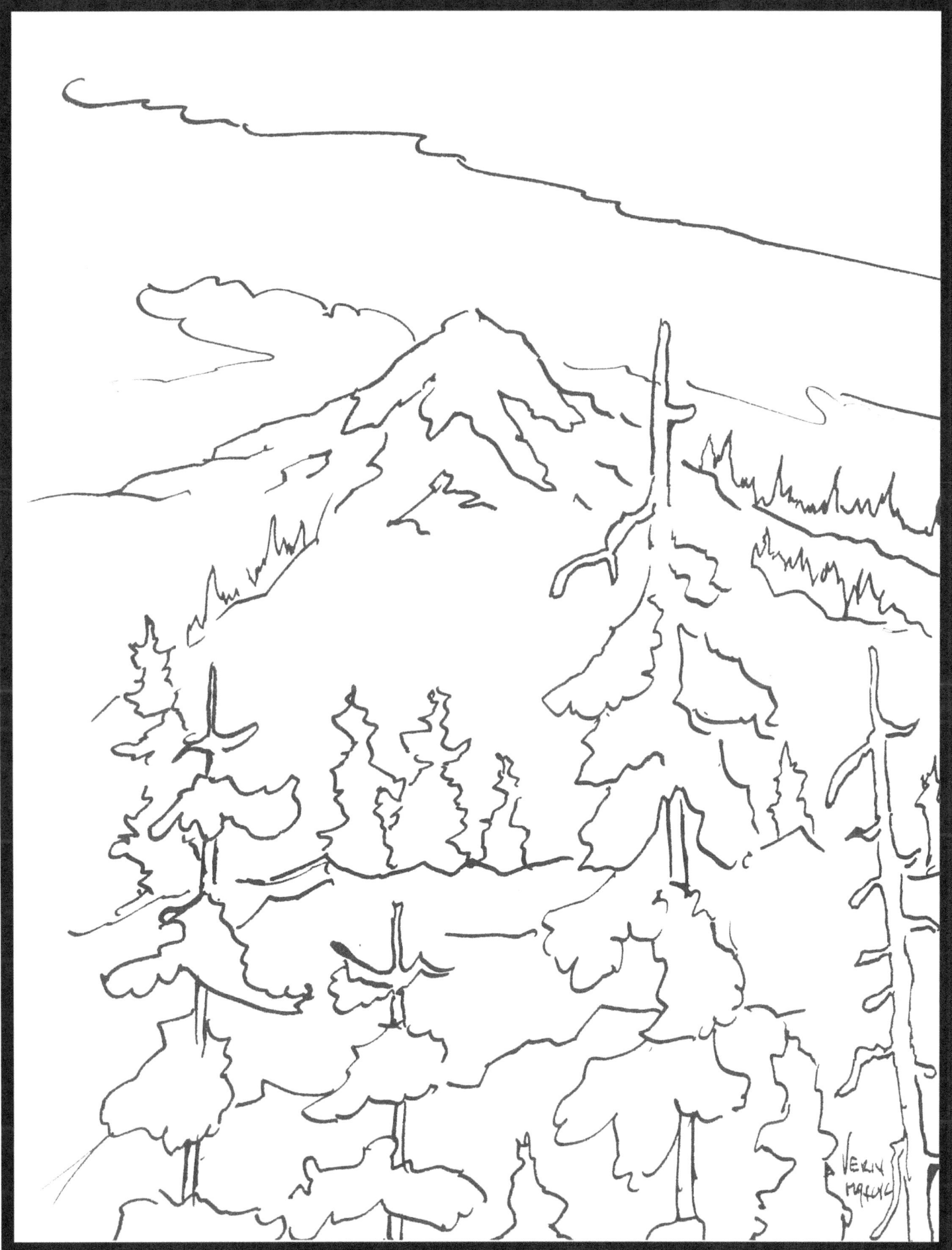

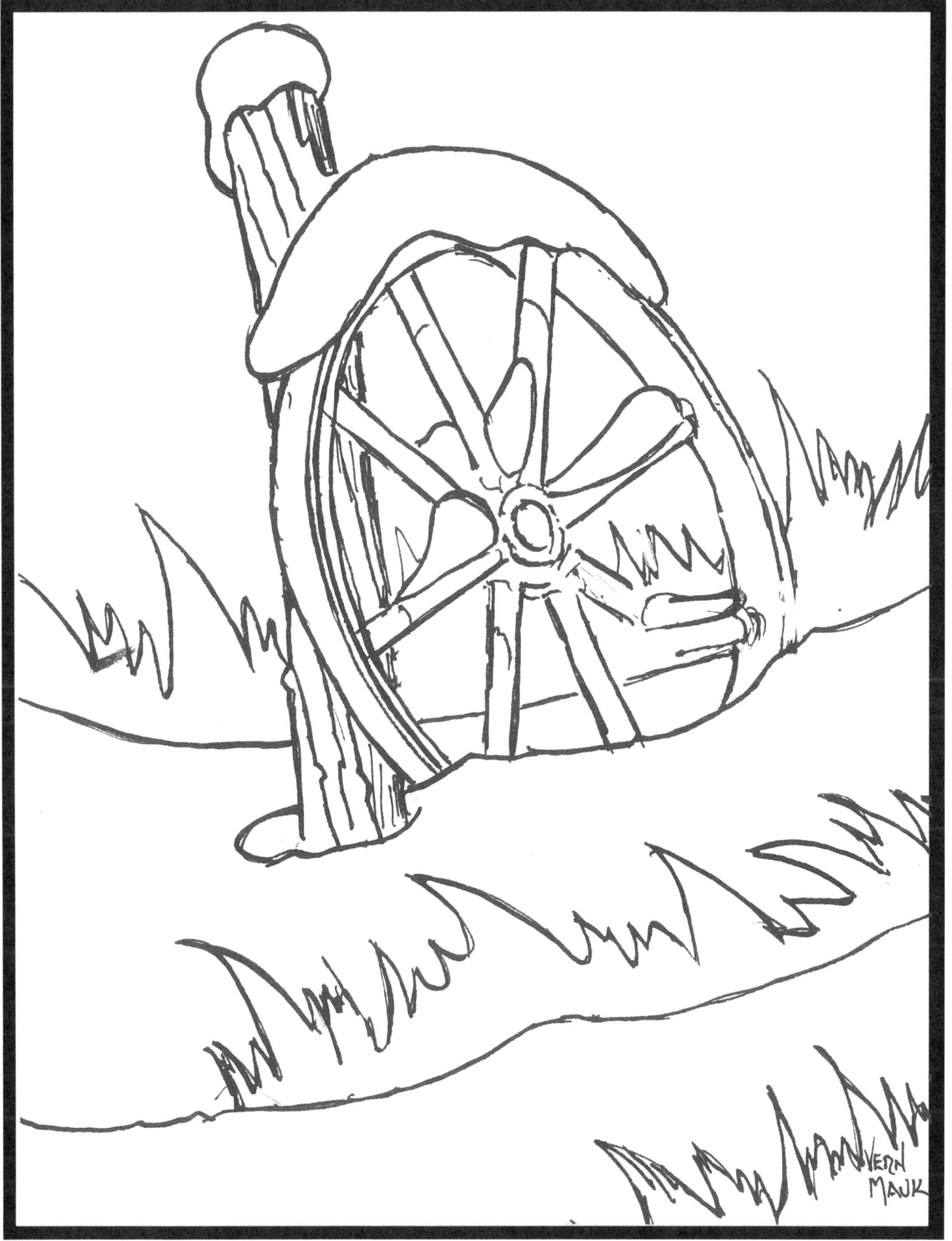

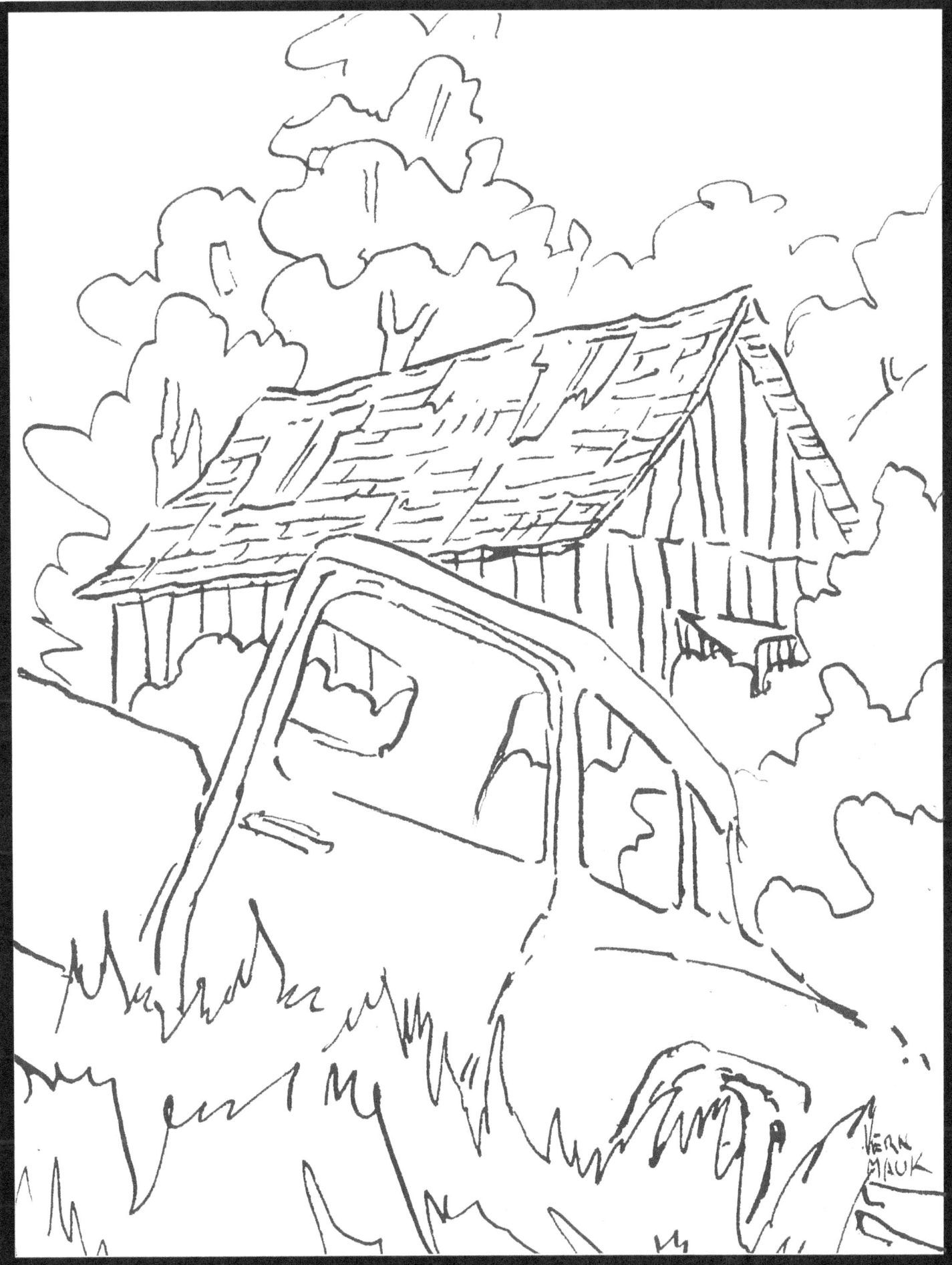

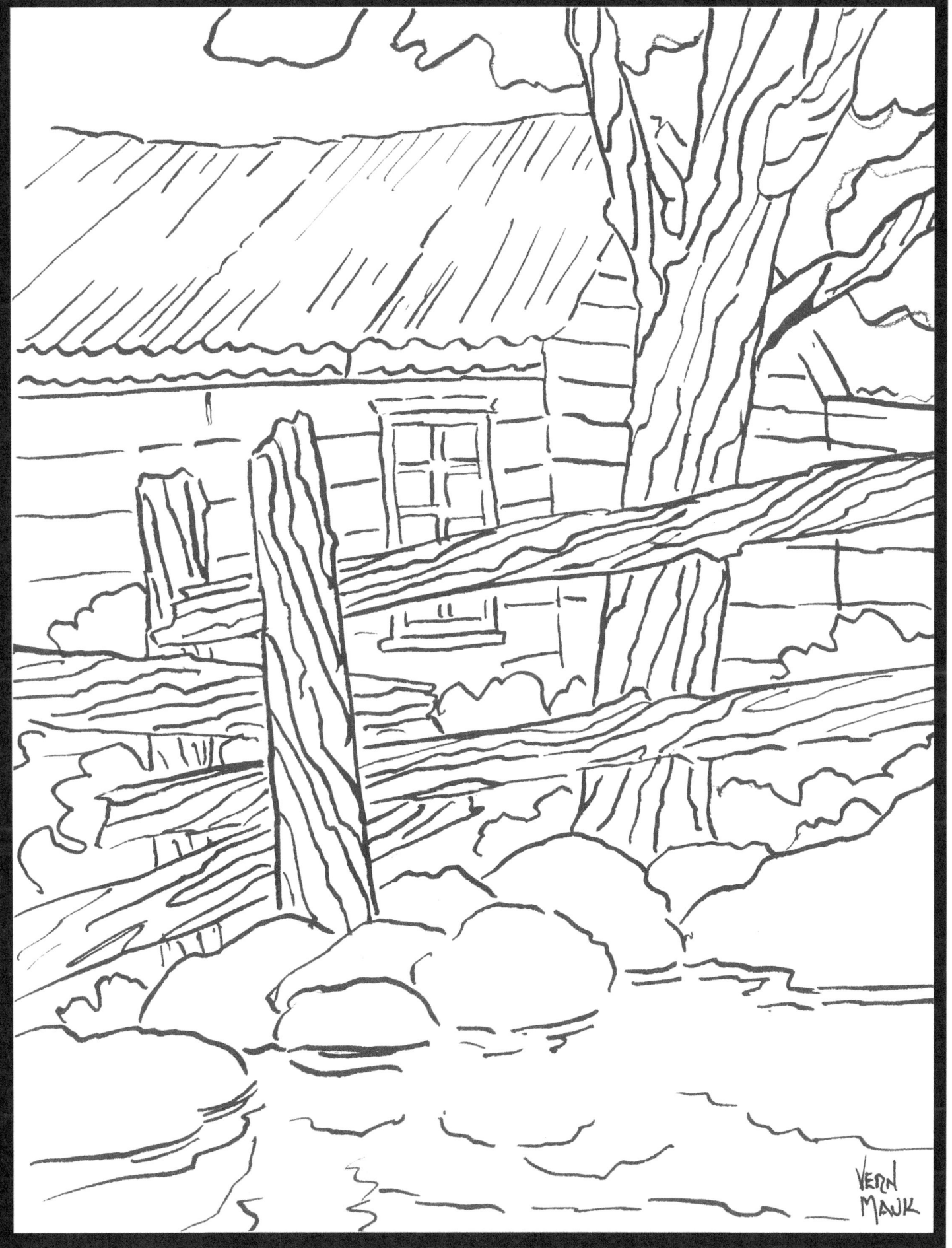

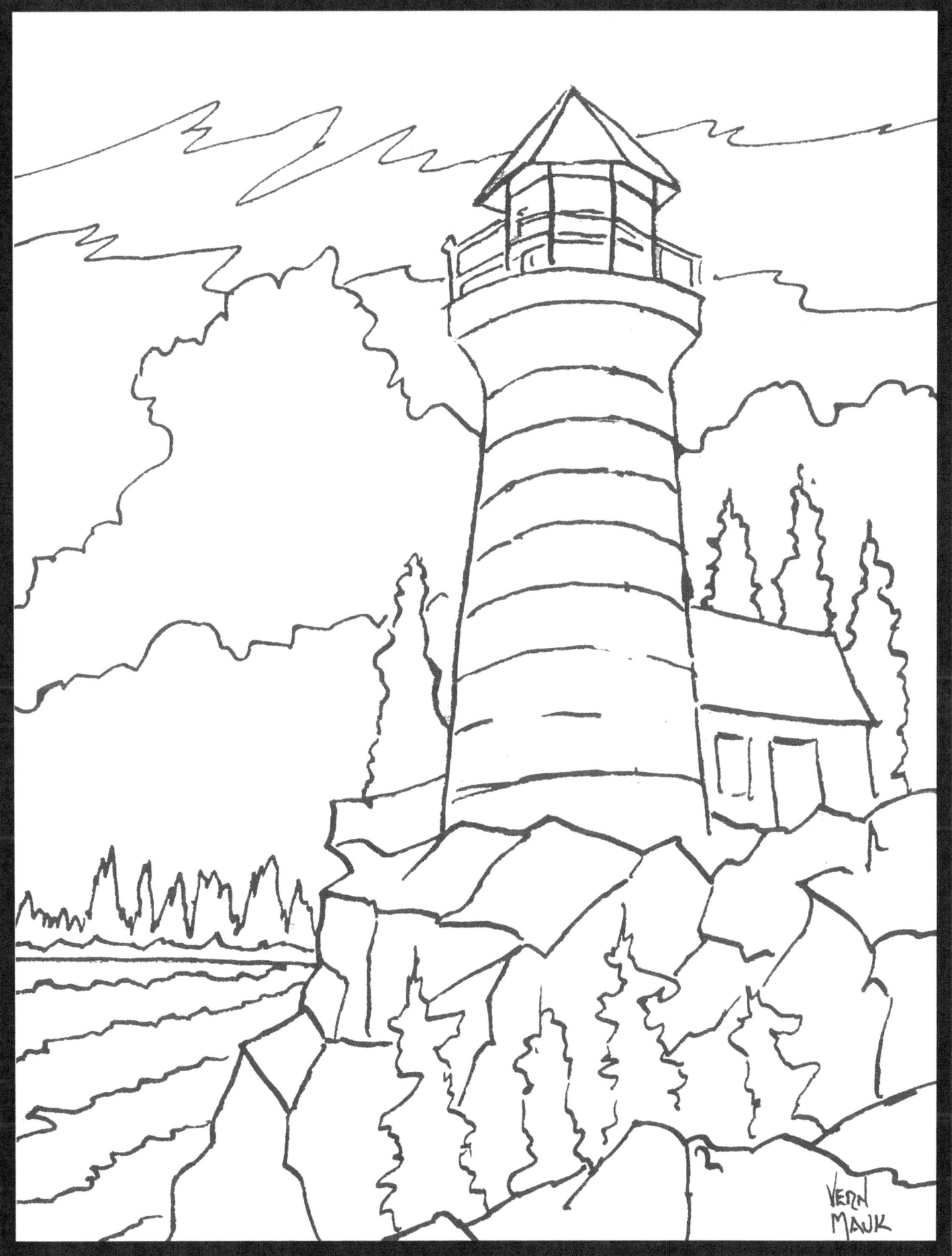

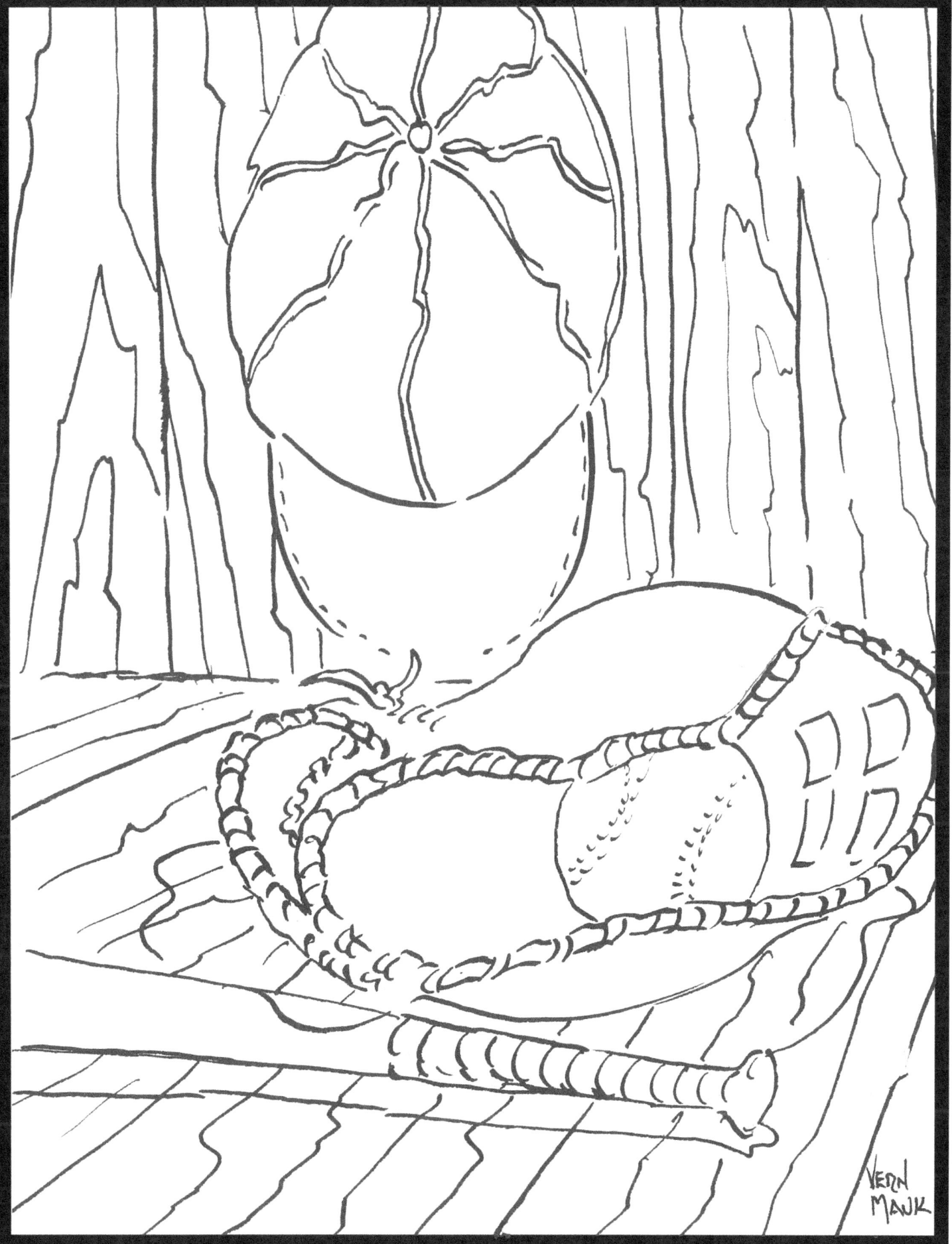

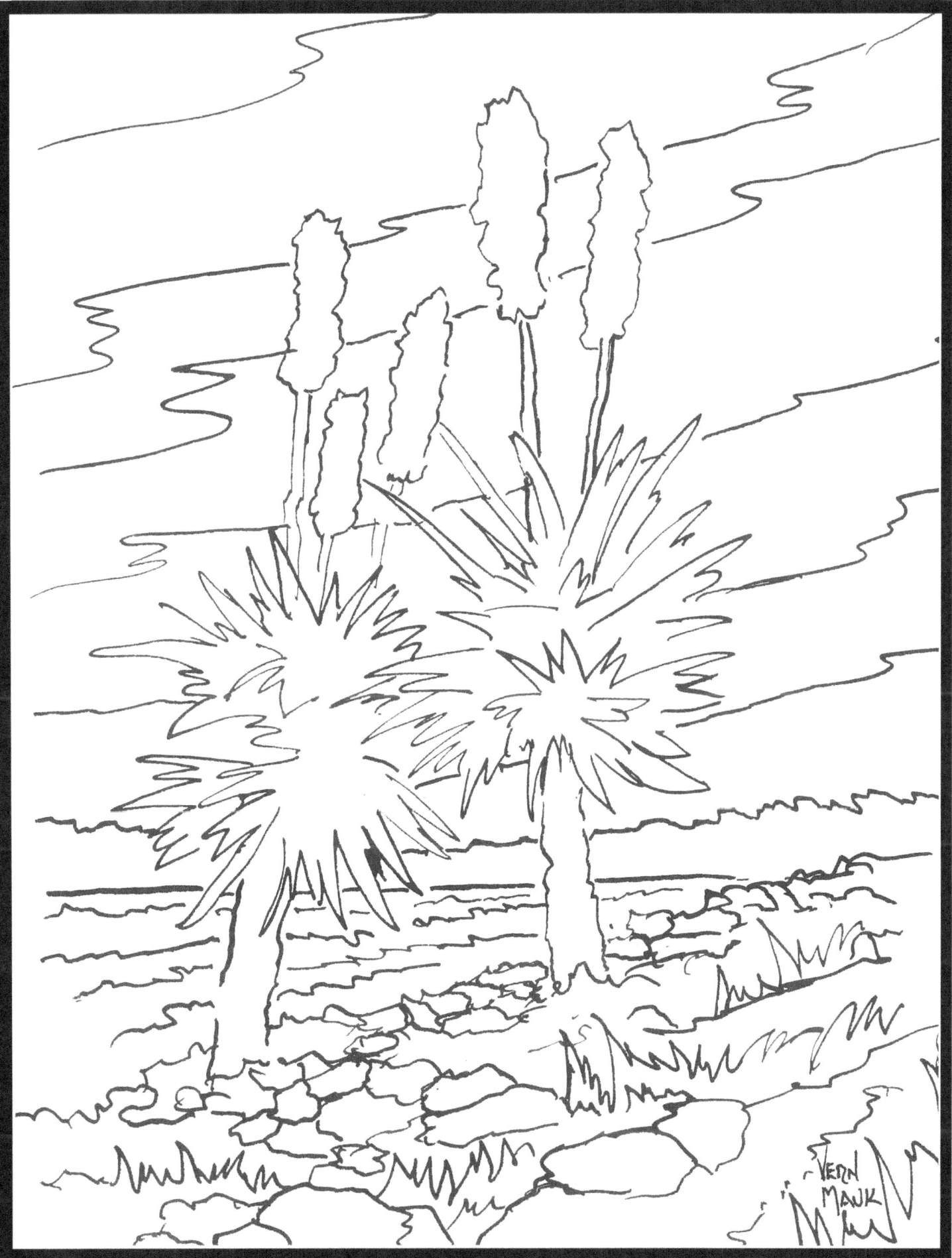

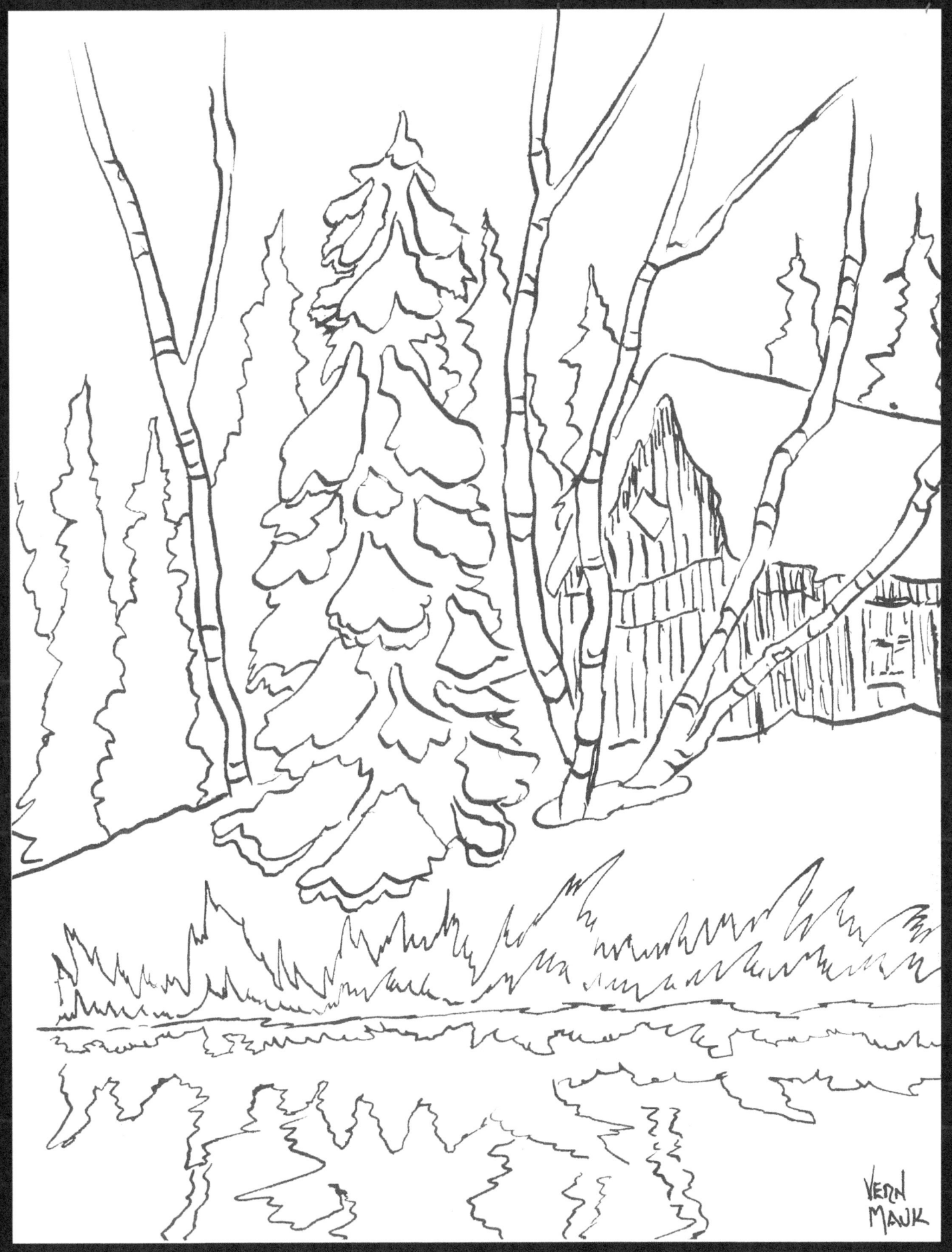

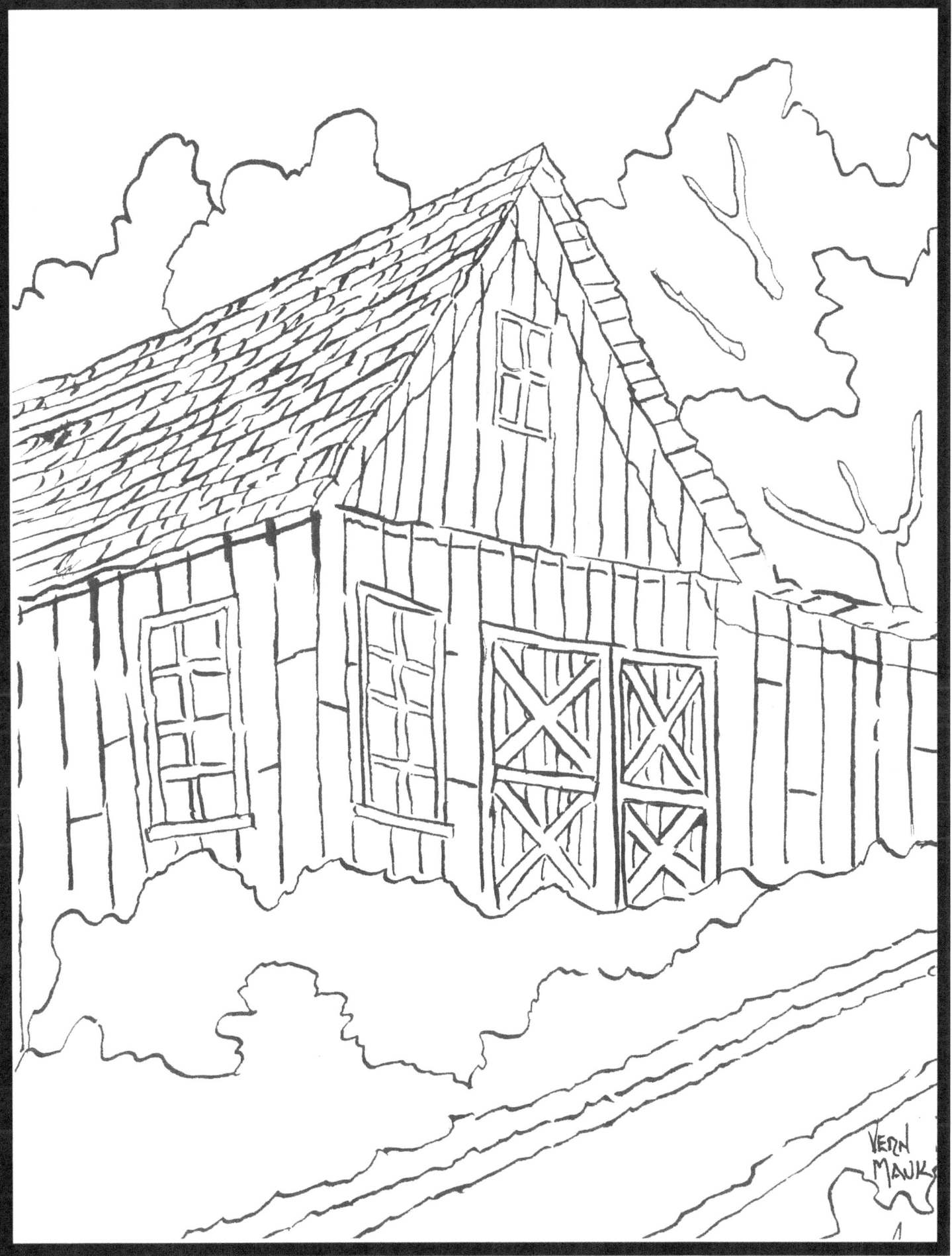

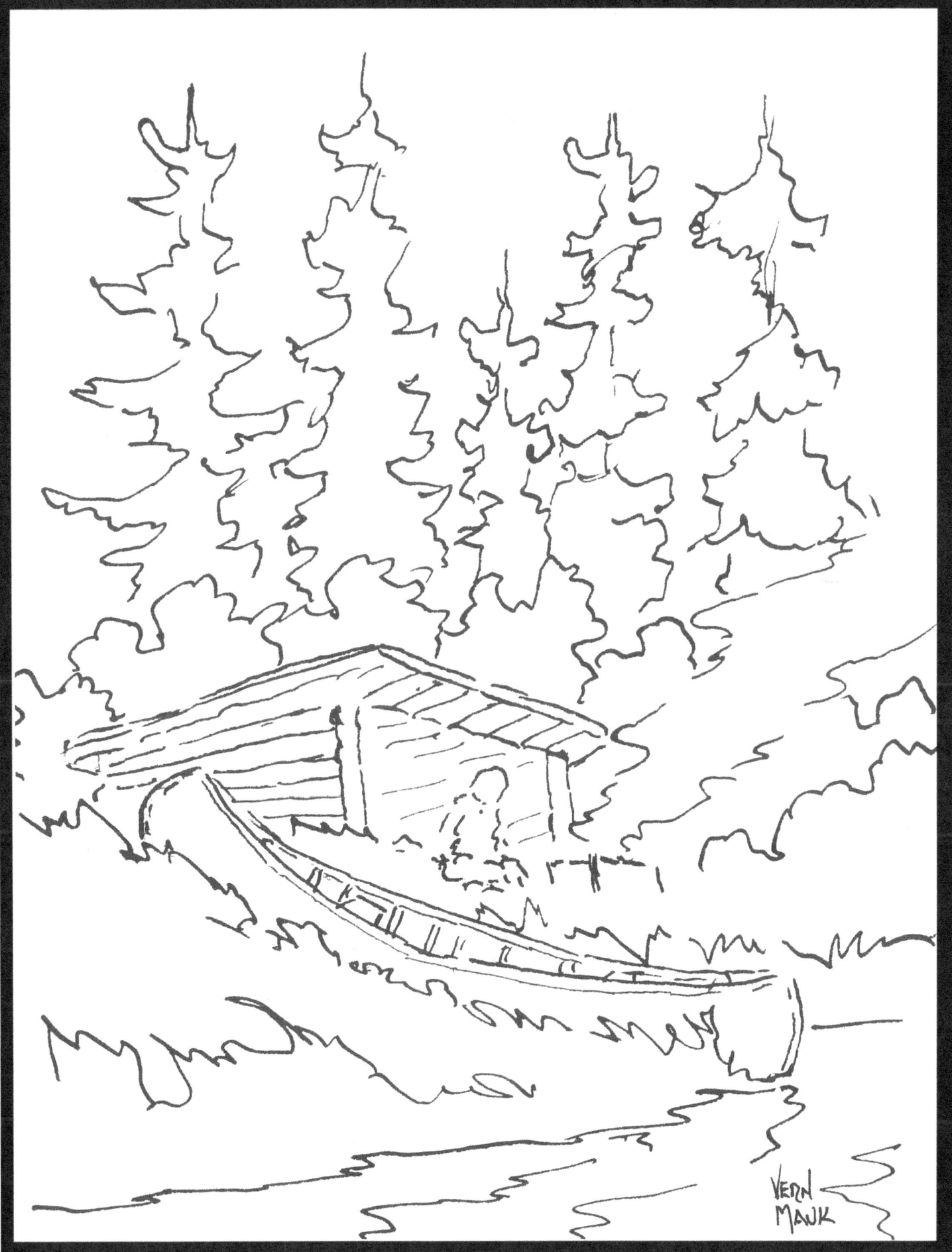

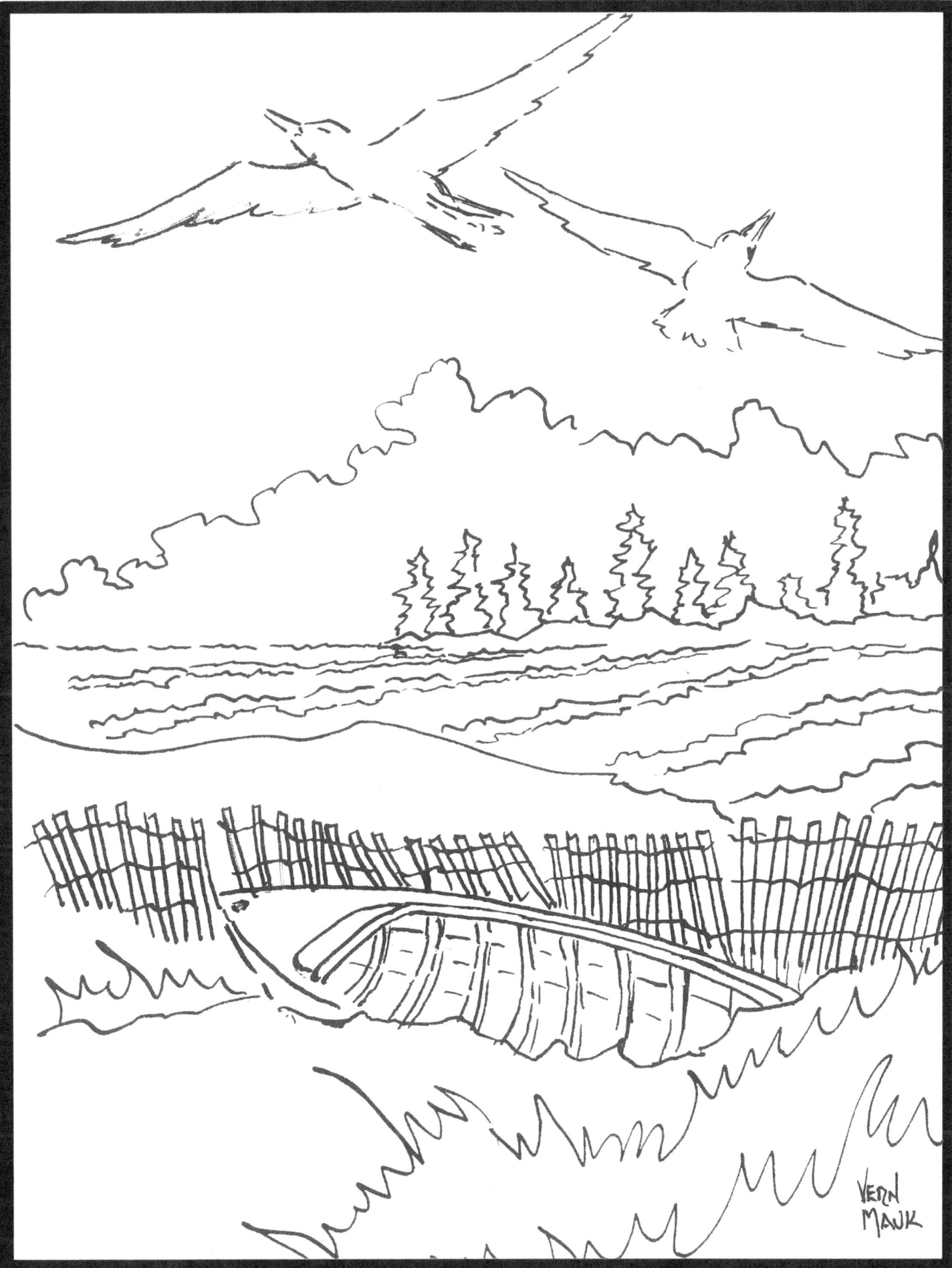

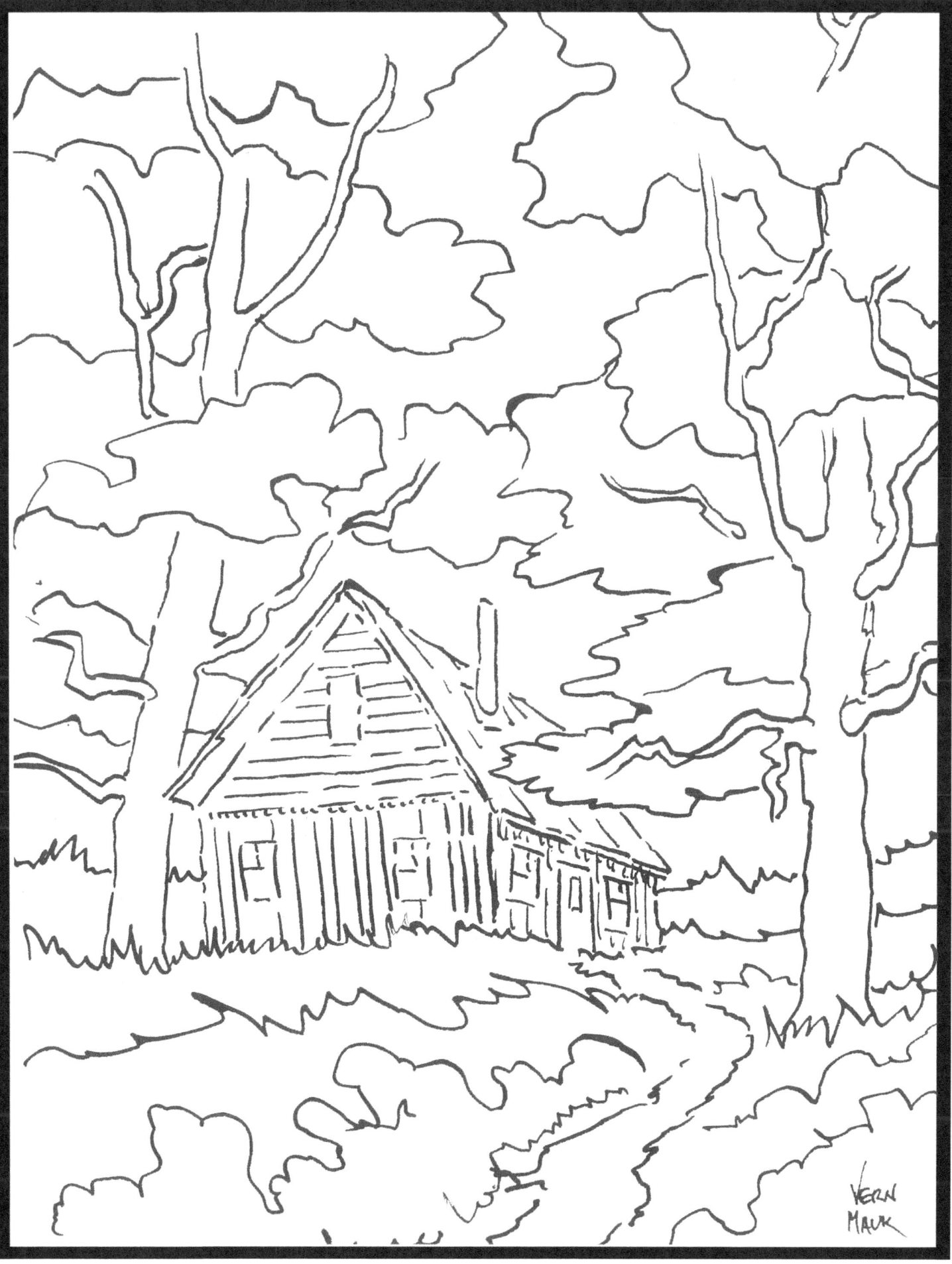

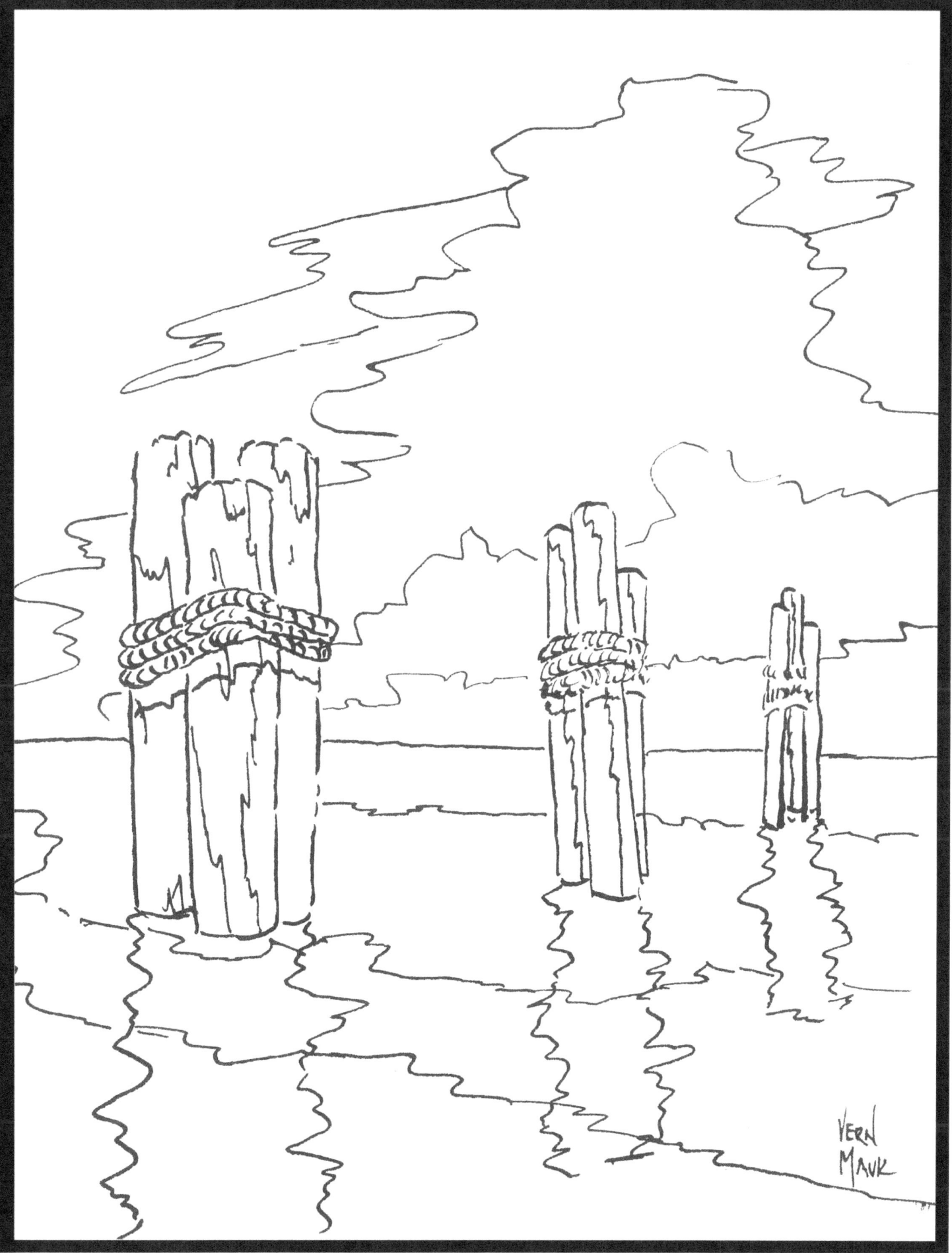

Vern Mauk's natural talents have been enhanced by his educational experiences. He hold a Bachelor's degree from Indiana State Teachers College (now Indiana University of Pennsylvania) and a Masters degree from Penn State U. Vern gives much credit to other artists who have influenced his work. Students also provide ideas and stimulation.

Vern's special interest is water color painting but he also works in oils and acrylics. Stained glass fasciantes him. He designed and supervised the making of several windows in the small chapel he built in memory of his son. He considers these windows to be his legacy.

Motorcycling, flying, skiing, table tennis, and race walking are ongoing activities. He is also an avid reader. Vern maintains a studio and gallery with his wife in Massena, NY where his original art can be seen.

www.ingramcontent.com/pod-product-compliance
Lightning Source LLC
Chambersburg PA
CBHW080133240526
45468CB00009BA/2421